SCHOLASTIC

Follow-the-Directions
No-Cook Snacks

by Immacula A. Rhodes

NEW YORK • TORONTO • LONDON • AUCKLAND • SYDNEY
MEXICO CITY • NEW DELHI • HONG KONG • BUENOS AIRES

Teaching *Resources*

To Amber and Alan:

You add spice to my life!

Taste and see that the LORD is good;

blessed is the man who takes refuge in him.

PSALM 34:8 (NIV)

Cover design by Maria Lilja
Interior design by Kathy Massaro
Illustrations by Bari Weissman

ISBN: 978-0-545-20824-6

Copyright © 2012 by Immacula A. Rhodes
Illustrations © 2012 by Scholastic Inc.
All rights reserved. Published by Scholastic Inc.
Printed in the U.S.A.

3 4 5 6 7 8 9 10   40   19 18 17 16 15 14 13

Contents

No-Cook Recipes

🍁 Fall

❄ Winter

❀ Spring

🐚 Summer

✿ ☆ Anytime

About This Book

Combine nutritious, no-cook ingredients with simple text, stir in supportive illustrations, flavor with a dash of fine motor skills, and...*voila*! You have the perfect recipe for delicious, snack-time learning! *Follow-the-Directions No-Cook Snacks* is a collection of tasty recipes designed to introduce children to healthy food choices and boost beginning reading skills.

These fun-to-make snacks—connected to seasonal and holiday themes—use healthy, low-cost ingredients that are easy to gather and prepare. Step-by-step recipe cards feature easy-to-read directions paired with simple art, providing children the support they need to make each snack independently and successfully. The snack-making activities give children practice in important reading skills, such as word recognition, using context clues, and demonstrating comprehension. In addition, each set of recipe cards can be assembled into a mini-book to help reinforce comprehension through sequencing while also building fine motor skills. Related extension activities offer additional ways to teach and build reading skills and expand children's learning opportunities.

Each lesson is designed to meet students' needs—academically and nutritionally—by incorporating reading with purpose with creating healthy snacks. The activities align with the English/Language Arts standards outlined by the Common Core State Standards Initiative for students in kindergarten and grade 1. (See page 7.) You can use the mini-books for whole-class activities or have children complete them with partners or in small groups after making their snacks. The books also work well as learning center or take-home activities.

With these tasty treats and meaningful mini-books, you'll find there's no better time than snack time to help children explore new flavors as they discover that reading can be both useful and fun.

What's Inside

Each lesson includes the following:

❋ **Introducing the Snack**

Use the activity here to make a connection between the holiday or special day and the snack children will make.

❋ **Ingredients**

Check this list to find out what you need for the recipe and how much is needed for each child.

❋ **Tools & Materials**

Gather the tools and materials needed for the recipe to have available for children's use.

❋ **Ahead of Time**

These suggestions let you know what and how to prepare in advance of making the snack.

❋ **Helpful Tips**

You'll find tips here that offer ways to make the ingredients easy to use and suggestions for making substitutions.

❋ **Extending the Learning**

In this section, you'll find activities that link the snack topic to important reading skills, such as phonics, vocabulary, and comprehension.

❋ **Mini-Book**

The reproducible mini-book includes step-by-step directions for making the snack. The predictable format, simple text, and user-friendly art offer support at each stage to help children follow the directions and complete the snack independently.

Preparing the Snacks

Color and cut out a copy of the recipe cards for the snack you want children to make. (Cut off the glue tabs for use as individual cards.) If desired, use an enlarged copy of the cards. Number the steps and laminate the cards. Post them, in sequence, in your snack-making center. Next, set out the ingredients, placing them from left to right and trying to keep each one near the recipe card that shows how to use that ingredient. Then point out and name each ingredient. Finally, read aloud and model each step to make the snack. You might also display a snack that you made in advance so children can see what the end result will be as they observe the snack coming together step by step. After the demonstration, review the steps once again to reinforce comprehension and invite questions or comments.

Tips for Success

❋ For recipes that require cookie cutters, gather several to have on hand for children's use.

❋ You might "go green" by using recyclable containers and utensils that can be washed and reused.

❋ When making the snack with the whole class at the same time, form small groups, then provide a dish of each ingredient for the children in each group to share.

❋ If an ingredient is not in a labeled container, add a label to help children identify it.

❋ A few days in advance, you might send a note home to parents and caregivers requesting specific ingredients for the recipe you'll be using. If desired, ask that they prepare the ingredients for use before sending them in. For instance, they might send in sliced carrots or chopped bell pepper.

❋ Solicit the help of parents or volunteers to come in early and prepare the ingredients on the day children will make the snack. You might also arrange for them to stay and help with the snack-making activity as well as clean up afterward.

Making the Mini-Books

After children make and enjoy their snack, give them a copy of the corresponding mini-book pattern and have them follow these simple directions to assemble their book. They can read their completed books with partners at school, then take them home to read and to make the snack with their families.

1 Cut out the three sets of mini-book pages. (There are two pages in each set).

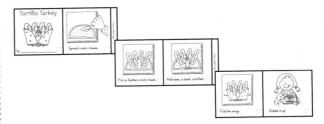

2 Sequence the pages, using the picture and text clues as guides. Write in the number for each step. Then color the pictures.

3 Glue the pages together where indicated.

4 Fold the pages to make an accordion-fold book.

Optional Assembly: Cut apart all of the mini-book pages (trim off the glue tabs). Sequence the pages, fill in the page numbers, and color the art. Stack and staple the pages together along the left edge.

Follow-the-Directions: No-Cook Snacks © 2012 by Immacula A. Rhodes, Scholastic Teaching Resources

Customized Recipe Cards

If you have your own snack creation to share with children, use the template on page 64 to make a set of recipe cards for the snack. You can draw simple sketches and use easy-to-read text for each step. Or, for art, take digital photos of each step, size the images to fit the cards, and glue each one to the appropriate card.

Teaching With the Recipe Cards

Use these quick-and-easy activities to reinforce reading with the recipe cards.

❋ Give children a set of unnumbered recipe cards to read and sequence. When finished, children pass their cards, in sequence, to a partner to check their work.

❋ Place the recipe cards (unnumbered) in random order in a pocket chart. Ask children if the directions make sense. Then have them put the cards in the correct order.

❋ Point out sight words on a word wall, such as *a, and, on, put, small, the,* and *two.* Then have children search the recipe cards for matching words.

❋ Mix up the recipe cards from a few different snacks. Challenge children to sort and sequence the cards for each of the snacks.

Health and Safety Guidelines

❋ Always check for food allergies, sensitivities, or restrictions before having children complete a snack. Adjust recipes, make substitutions, or omit an ingredient (if possible), for children who have special dietary requirements.

❋ Before working with the recipes, wash your hands well—and have children do the same. You might also use hand sanitizer or antibacterial, pre-moistened hand wipes.

❋ In advance, thoroughly wash and dry all fruits and vegetables. Take exceptional care with unpeeled foods that will be used in the recipes, such as bell peppers, cucumbers, zucchini, and squash.

❋ Always prepare food on a clean, sanitized surface. You might use disinfecting wipes to clean surfaces before and after use.

❋ To keep ingredients fresh and ready to use, store them in airtight containers or resealable plastic bags.

❋ Leave perishables, such as cream cheese spread and yogurt, in the refrigerator for as long as possible before use. Return any unused portions to the refrigerator as soon as possible.

❋ Always use clean utensils for snack preparation. When measuring or serving a portion from a larger container, have children use a designated utensil—such as a spoon or tongs—to remove what they need. They can then use their own utensils to complete their snack.

Connections to the Common Core State Standards

The Common Core State Standards Initiative (CCSSI) has outlined learning expectations in English/Language Arts for students at different grade levels. The activities in this book align with the following standards for students in kindergarten and grade 1. For more information, visit the CCSSI Web site at www.corestandards.org.

Reading Standards for Informational Text

Key Ideas and Details

- RI.K.1, RI.1.1. Ask and answer questions about key details in a text.

- RI.K.2, RI.1.2. Identify the main topic and retell key details of a text.

- RI.K.3, RI.1.3. Describe the connection between two ideas or pieces of information in a text.

Craft and Structure

- RI.K.4, RI.1.4. Ask and answer questions to help determine or clarify the meaning of words and phrases in a text.

- RI.1.6. Distinguish between information provided by pictures or other illustrations and information provided by the words in a text.

Integration of Knowledge and Ideas

- RI.K.7, RI.1.7. Use the illustrations and details in a text to describe its key ideas.

Range of Reading and Level of Text Complexity

- RI.K.10. Actively engage in group reading activities with purpose and understanding.

- RI.1.10. With prompting and support, read informational texts appropriately complex for grade 1.

Reading Standards: Foundational Skills

Print Concepts

- RF.K.1, RF.1.1. Demonstrate understanding of the organization and basic features of print.

Phonological Awareness

- RF.K.2, RF1.2. Demonstrate understanding of spoken words, syllables, and sounds (phonemes).

Phonics and Word Recognition

- RF.K.3, RF.1.3. Know and apply grade-level phonics and word analysis skills in decoding words.

Fluency

- RF.K.4. Read emergent-reader texts with purpose and understanding.

- RF.1.4. Read with sufficient accuracy and fluency to support comprehension.

MyPlate

Use the MyPlate place-setting image provided by the United States Department of Agriculture (USDA) to help children identify which food groups their snack ingredients fit into. For more information about the five food groups, tips for building healthier diets, or to find a downloadable version of the MyPlate image, visit http://www.choosemyplate.gov.

Wheat Bread Bus

Roll into a discussion about bus safety with this nutritious snack.

Introducing the Snack

Display a picture of a school bus. Point out the safety features of the bus, such as the flashing lights, stop sign, and swinging arm. Talk about how each feature helps make the bus safe. Then tell children that they will make a bus-shaped snack complete with its own stop sign. After enjoying their snack, invite children to make the corresponding mini-book.

Ahead of Time

- Use a sharp knife to cut one slice of bread in half vertically for every two children.
- Cut small grape tomatoes crosswise into thin slices for the stop signs.
- Break pretzel sticks into $\frac{1}{2}$-inch lengths for the stop sign handles.

Helpful Tips

- Rounded-top bread works well for this snack.
- If desired, use whole-grain bread.

Ingredients
(for each child)

- $\frac{1}{2}$ slice of wheat bread
- pimento cheese
- 4 Rice Chex® cereal squares
- slice of small grape tomato
- short piece of pretzel stick
- 2 large olive slices

Tools & Materials
(for each child)

- mini-book pattern (page 9)
- napkin
- plastic knife

Extending the Learning

Work with the class to generate a list of bus safety rules. After discussing, invite children to make up verses to "The Wheels on the Bus" that tell about safe ways to ride. For example, they might sing "The children on the bus stay in their seats." For additional verses, they might complete the line "The children on the bus…" with "talk quietly," "keep hands to self," "walk carefully," or "follow the rules."

Follow-the-Directions: No-Cook Snacks © 2012 by Immacula A. Rhodes, Scholastic Teaching Resources

Wheat Bread Bus

by _____

Spread pimento cheese.

Glue page 3 here.

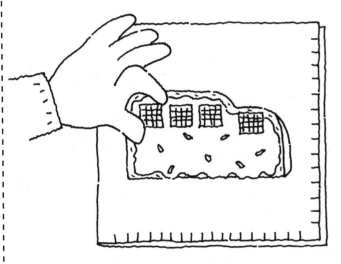

Put on the windows.

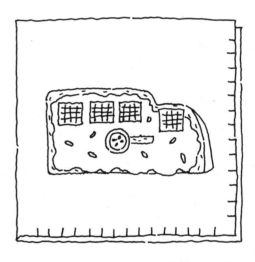

Add the stop sign and handle.

Glue page 5 here.

Put on the wheels.

Beep! Beep!

Here comes the bus!

Crunchy Apple Basket

Celebrate the fall harvest with this tasty apple-basket treat.

Introducing the Snack

Fall is apple-picking time! Bring in an apple to show children. Then cut it open to reveal the seeds inside. Explain that new apple trees can grow from the small seeds. Next, work with children to trace the development of an apple backwards—from ripe fruit to bloom to bud and so on to its beginning as a tiny seed. Afterward, tell children that they will make an edible basket filled with apple-y treats. Finally, invite them to make the corresponding mini-book.

Ahead of Time

- Chop unpeeled apples into small pieces.
- For basket handles, cut $\frac{1}{4}$-inch wide strips from individually wrapped strawberry or cherry all-natural fruit strips, such as Stretch Island Fruit Co.™ Original Fruit Strips. Each strip should be about 4 inches in length. You can make 6 handles from each fruit strip.

Helpful Tips

- Taper each end of the fruit strips to resemble an arrow point. This will help children fit the ends more easily into the ice cream cone.
- If all-natural fruit strips are not available, you might use a length of red licorice rope for the handle.

Ingredients
(for each child)

- flat-bottom ice cream cone
- chopped red apples
- 1 tablespoon applesauce
- $\frac{1}{4}$-inch wide all-natural fruit strip

Tools & Materials
(for each child)

- mini-book pattern (page 11)
- napkin
- plastic knife

Harvest a crop of letters to reinforce alphabet recognition skills. First, label apple cutouts with letters of the alphabet. Use all capital letters, all lowercase letters, or a combination of the two. Then make a large tree from bulletin board paper. Display the tree on a wall and add the apple cutouts. (You might put some in the tree, on the ground, and even in an apple basket cutout.) Finally, invite children to "pick" the apples and name the letters.

Crunchy Apple Basket

by _____

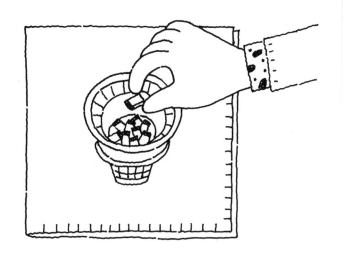

Put apples in the cone.

Add applesauce.

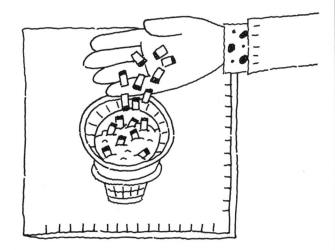

Put more apples on top.

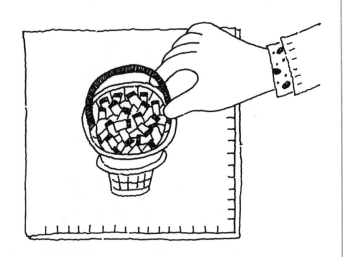

Add the handle.

A-tisket, a-tasket,
a crunchy apple basket!

Follow-the-Directions: No-Cook Snacks © 2012 by Immacula A. Rhodes, Scholastic Teaching Resources • PAGE 11

Glue page 3 here.

Glue page 5 here.

Fall Tree

Greet fall with this crunchable tree creation.

Fall Tree | by _____ | Spread hummus. | Put on short limbs. | Put on long limbs. | Add leaves. | It's a tree treat!

Ingredients
(for each child)

- 4-inch length of celery stalk
- hummus
- 6 chow mein noodles
- bran flakes

Tools & Materials
(for each child)

- mini-book pattern (page 13)
- napkin
- plastic knife

Introducing the Snack

Ask children to describe what happens to the leaves on trees in the fall. Help them understand that the leaves change colors—eventually turning brown—and then fall off the trees, leaving bare branches by the end of the season. If desired, show children a few colorful fall leaves along with images of leaf-shedding trees at different stages. After your discussion, tell children that they will make a crunchy fall-tree snack. After children eat their snack, invite them to make the corresponding mini-book.

Ahead of Time

- Cut celery stalks into 4-inch lengths.
- Break chow mein noodles into various lengths to use for limbs on the tree.

Helpful Tips

- Strip the strings from the celery stalks to make them easier for children to chew.
- If desired, substitute peanut butter for hummus.
- Encourage children to place the shorter limbs at the top of their tree trunk, and the longer ones closer to the bottom.

Extending the Learning

Cut out pictures of items that begin with eight to ten different letters of the alphabet. Choose at least three pictures for each letter. (Look for pictures in old magazines, sales flyers, workbooks, or clip-art programs.) Glue the pictures onto leaf cutouts in fall colors—one picture per leaf. To use, show children one leaf at a time, naming the picture on it. Ask them to identify the letter that begins each word. Later, put the leaves in a center for children to sort by beginning sounds.

Follow-the-Directions: No-Cook Snacks © 2012 by Immacula A. Rhodes, Scholastic Teaching Resources

Fall Tree

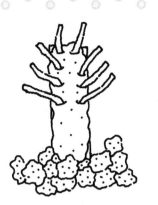

by _____

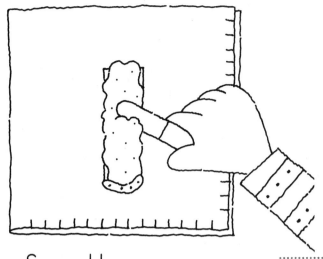

Spread hummus.

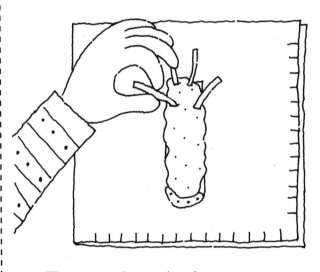

Put on short limbs.

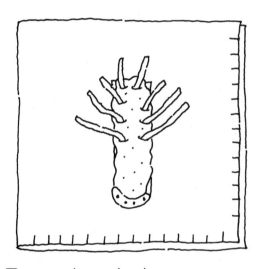

Put on long limbs.

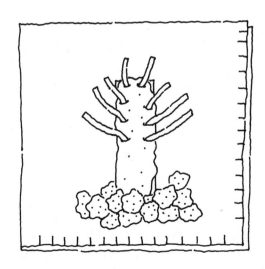

Add leaves.

It's a tree treat!

Columbus Day Ship

Invite kids to enjoy this ship-shape snack on Columbus Day.

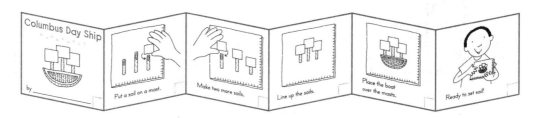

Ingredients
(for each child)

- orange wedge (cut from a seedless orange)
- 3 pretzel sticks
- 3 small cheese squares (cut from individually wrapped slices of Swiss cheese)
- cream cheese spread

Tools & Materials
(for each child)

- mini-book pattern (page 15)
- napkin
- plastic knife

Introducing the Snack

"In fourteen hundred and ninety-two, Columbus sailed the ocean blue." Share this rhyme with children, then talk about what it means. Explain that Christopher Columbus and his crew sailed from Spain to the "New World" in 1492. His ships were named *Niña*, *Pinta*, and *Santa Maria*. Show children images of ships that were used during that time. Then tell them that they will make their own sailing ship for a snack. Afterward, invite children to make the corresponding mini-book.

Ahead of Time

- Cut oranges into six wedges. One orange can be used for six children.
- Create sets of three pretzel sticks for each child. Break two pretzel sticks into smaller lengths to make the shorter masts for the ship.
- Cut each slice of Swiss cheese into four smaller squares. Three slices will make enough sails for four children.

Helpful Tips

- Invite children to make their ship on a blue napkin or 6-inch paper plate to represent the sea.
- If seedless oranges aren't available, remove the seeds from the wedges before children make the snack.
- Use cream cheese spread as "glue" to hold the sails in place on the masts.
- Use grapefruit wedges (seedless) to give the ship a different size, color, and flavor.

Extending the Learning

Label a supply of simple ship cutouts with word-family endings. Then write words that belong to each word family on white sail cutouts. Put all of the cutouts in a center along with a supply of craft sticks. Invite children to the center to sort the sails by word-family endings. They can then put the sails on the corresponding ship, using the craft sticks as masts. (If desired, provide removable adhesive for children to use to hold the ships together.)

Columbus Day Ship

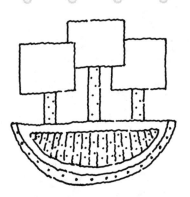

by _____

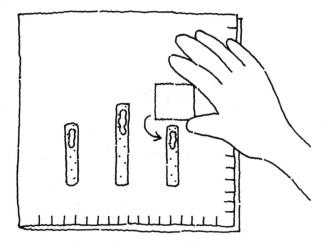

Put a sail on a mast.

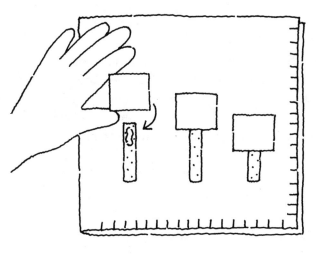

Make two more sails.

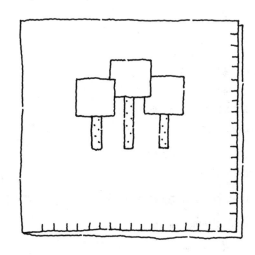

Line up the sails.

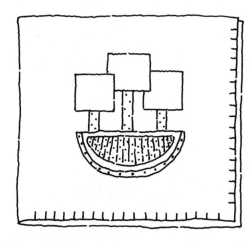

Place the boat
over the masts.

Ready to set sail!

Glue page 3 here.

Glue page 5 here.

Creepy Cracker Spider

Kids will go buggy over this fun and filling spider treat.

Ingredients
(for each child)

- large, round wheat cracker
- small, round wheat cracker
- red-pepper hummus
- 8 chow mein noodles
- two raisins

Tools & Materials
(for each child)

- mini-book pattern (page 17)
- napkin
- plastic knife

Introducing the Snack

Sing "The Itsy-Bitsy Spider" with children (or read a book version of the song). Then invite children to share what they know about spiders. During the discussion, share facts and additional information that you know about spiders. If desired, display images of different kinds of spiders and point out that they all have eight legs. Wrap up by telling children that they will make a crunchy spider to enjoy for snack. Afterward, invite them to make the corresponding mini-book.

Ahead of Time

Sort out chow mein noodles that are shaped appropriately for use as spider legs.

Helpful Tips

- Baked wheat crackers such as Dare Breton originals ($2\frac{1}{2}$-inch) and mini baked bite-size ($1\frac{1}{4}$-inch) crackers work well for the spider body and head.
- Use plain hummus or a cheese spread to give the spider a different color or flavor.

Label several spider cutouts with beginning consonant blends, such as *cl, dr, gl, pr, sc, sp,* and *tr.* Display the spiders across the top of a sheet of chart paper, chalkboard, or whiteboard. Then work with children to brainstorm words that begin with each blend. Write each word under the corresponding spider. Afterward, review the lists of words, inviting children to take turns choosing a word and using it in a sentence.

Creepy Cracker Spider

by _____

Glue page 3 here.

Spread hummus.

Put on the head.

Put on 8 legs.

Glue page 5 here.

Add eyes.

Creepy, crawly, crunchy!

Tortilla Turkey

This turkey snack struts healthy ingredients from four food groups.

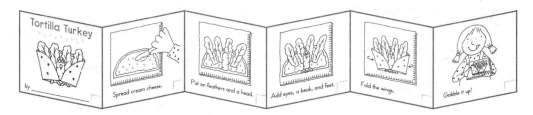

Ingredients
(for each child)

- $\frac{1}{2}$ six-inch flour tortilla
- 1 tablespoon cream cheese spread
- 4 lettuce leaf strips
- $\frac{1}{2}$ baby carrot, cut lengthwise
- 3 sunflower seeds
- 2 thin slices of celery

Tools & Materials
(for each child)

- mini-book pattern (page 19)
- napkin
- plastic knife

Introducing the Snack

Explain to children that the Pilgrims shared a feast with the Wampanoag in 1621 to give thanks for their bountiful harvest. Many foods were served at the feast, including turkey, deer, and dishes made from the grains and vegetables that the Pilgrims grew with the help of the Wampanoag. Today, the turkey is a common symbol of the Thanksgiving holiday. Then tell children that they will make a turkey snack using foods from four food groups: proteins, vegetables, dairy, and grains. Finally, invite them to make the corresponding mini-book.

Ahead of Time

- Cut one tortilla round in half for every two children.
- For tail feathers, cut or tear lettuce leaves into strips that are about $\frac{3}{4}$-inch wide and $2\frac{1}{2}$-inches long.
- Cut one baby carrot in half lengthwise for every two children.
- Cut off the rounded bottom of each carrot to make it flat—use this end for the bottom of the turkey's body.

Helpful Tips

- Warm the tortillas to room temperature to make folding the wings easier for children.
- Use a dot of cream cheese spread to "glue" the sunflower eyes and beak in place.
- If desired, replace the celery slices with green olive slices. You can cut each olive slice in half to make two feet.

Extending the Learning

For this listen-and-move activity, have children pretend to be turkeys sitting on nests. Call out "Turkey ____," filling in the blank with a rhyming word, such as "Durkey" or "Wurkey." Then hold up a letter card. If that letter begins the second word of the name, the turkeys rise up off their nests and strut around. If not, they remain seated. Continue displaying a different letter card until the correct letter is shown and the turkeys are strutting all about.

Follow-the-Directions: No-Cook Snacks © 2012 by Immacula A. Rhodes, Scholastic Teaching Resources

Tortilla Turkey

by _____

Glue page 3 here.

Spread cream cheese.

Put on feathers and a head.

Add eyes, a beak, and feet.

Glue page 5 here.

Fold the wings.

Gobble it up!

Holiday Candle

Light up the holidays with this uniquely nutritious candle.

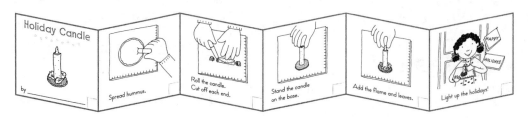

Introducing the Snack

Display pictures of different types of candleholders that are related to the winter holidays, such as an advent wreath, farolito, menorah, and kinara. Ask children to tell what the images have in common: candles (or light). Explain that many people use candles in their celebration of the winter holidays. Then invite children to share about how lights play a role in their holiday celebrations. Afterward, tell children that they will make a candle-shaped holiday snack. Finally, have them make the corresponding mini-book.

Ahead of Time

- If needed, shave the carrot tips to make them resemble the shape of candle flames.
- Tear lettuce leaves into thin, two- to three-inch long strips. Prepare three or four strips for each child to fit around the base of their candle (the leaves will overlap).

Helpful Tips

- You might help children cut off an inch or so from each end of the rolled tortilla.
- If desired, use a dab of hummus as "glue" to hold the candle upright and in place on the cracker.
- Lettuce leaves that have crepe-like or jagged edges work well for the greenery around the candle base.

Ingredients
(for each child)

- 6-inch flour tortilla
- hummus
- large, round wheat cracker
- $1\frac{1}{2}$-inch baby carrot tip
- torn lettuce leaves

Tools & Materials
(for each child)

- mini-book pattern (page 21)
- napkin
- plastic knife

Extending the Learning

To reinforce sight word recognition, label colorful candle cutouts with two- and three-letter sight words, such as *are, get, if, on, the,* and *you.* Use the candles to create a word wall. Then invite children to take turns pointing out a candle and reading the word on it. For additional practice, send children on a sight word scavenger hunt. Simply ask them to list any ten words from the word wall on paper, then search text sources around the classroom to find matching words.

Follow-the-Directions: No-Cook Snacks © 2012 by Immacula A. Rhodes, Scholastic Teaching Resources

Holiday Candle

by _____

Glue page 3 here.

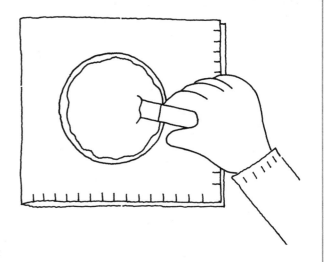

Spread hummus.

Roll the candle.
Cut off each end.

Glue page 5 here.

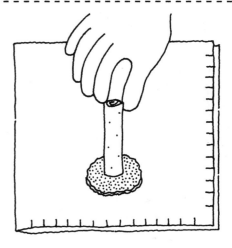

Stand the candle
on the base.

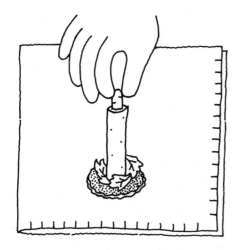

Add the flame and leaves.

Light up the holidays!

Winter Snowflake

This six-sided snowflake is the perfect winter wonderland treat.

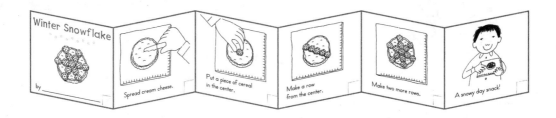

Ingredients
(for each child)

- rice cake
- cream cheese spread
- 13 pieces of Post Honeycomb® cereal

Tools & Materials
(for each child)

- mini-book pattern (page 23)
- napkin
- plastic knife

Introducing the Snack

Ask children to share what they know about snow. They might offer responses such as "snow is cold," "it comes in the winter," and "snowflakes fall from the sky." After sharing, tell children that all snowflakes are six-sided crystals—and that no two snowflakes are exactly alike! If desired, share more by reading aloud *Snowflake Bentley* by Jacqueline Briggs Martin (Sandpiper, 2009). Then tell children that they will make a tasty snowflake snack. Afterward, have them make the corresponding mini-book.

Ahead of Time

For younger children, you might group together the 13 pieces of cereal for each child.

Helpful Tips

- Let children practice placing the cereal pieces into a spoke-like arrangement before they create the design on the rice cake.
- If desired, substitute low-fat plain or vanilla yogurt for the cream cheese spread.

Build letter-sound discrimination skills with this activity. Label pairs of snowflake cutouts with two similarly spelled words that differ by only one letter, such as *bag* and *bug*, *map* and *mop*, and *net* and *not*. Place the snowflakes face up in a random arrangement. Then have children pair up the snowflakes labeled with similarly spelled words. Once finished, ask them to take turns choosing a snowflake pair, reading the words aloud, and then identifying the letter (and sound) that is different in the two words.

Follow-the-Directions: No-Cook Snacks © 2012 by Immacula A. Rhodes, Scholastic Teaching Resources

Winter Snowflake

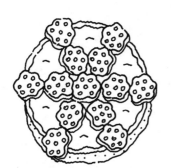

by _____

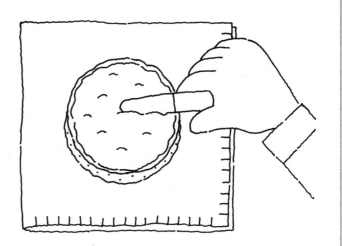

Spread cream cheese.

Glue page 3 here.

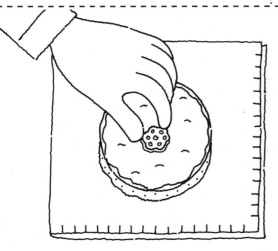

Put a piece of cereal
in the center.

Make a row
from the center.

Glue page 5 here.

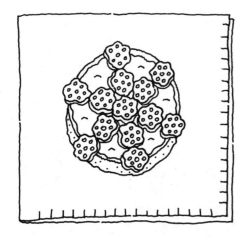

Make two more rows.

A snowy day snack!

Hibernating Bear

Snack time is snooze time for this tasty hibernating bear.

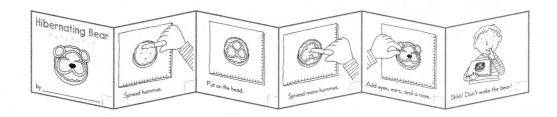

Ingredients
(for each child)

◆ mini-bagel half
◆ hummus
◆ pretzel twist
◆ 2 bagel chips
◆ 2 blanched almond slivers
◆ raisin

Tools & Materials
(for each child)

◆ mini-book pattern (page 25)
◆ napkin
◆ plastic knife

Introducing the Snack

Explain to children that, during winter, some animals migrate, some hibernate, and some stay active. Create a chart divided into the three categories. Then invite children to share what they know about animals that engage in each of these wintertime activities. List animals on the chart that belong to each category, including bears for hibernation. When finished, tell children that they will make a hibernating bear for snack. Afterward, have them make the corresponding mini-book.

Ahead of Time

Slice each mini-bagel in half crosswise to create a round top and bottom half. One bagel can be used for every two children.

Helpful Tips

◆ Use pretzel twists that measure about $2\frac{1}{2}$ inches across.
◆ If desired, substitute peanut butter or almond butter for the hummus.

To give children practice in rhyme-recognition skills, have them pretend to be hibernating bears. Tell them that you will call out one word at a time, such as *hear, hair, stare, stir, fear,* and *fair,* and if the word rhymes with *bear,* they will wake up, yawn and stretch, and move about like a bear on all fours. If the word does not rhyme, they will remain asleep. If desired, extend the activity by using other bear-related words, such as *roar, den,* and *fur.*

Hibernating Bear

by _____

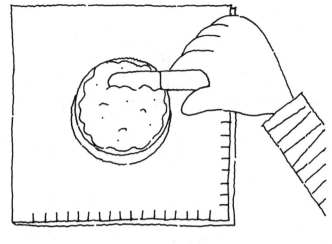

Spread hummus.

Glue page 3 here.

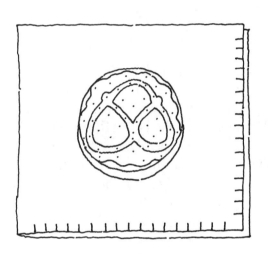

Put on the head.

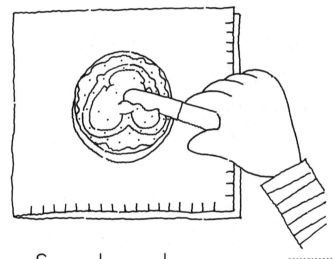

Spread more hummus.

Glue page 5 here.

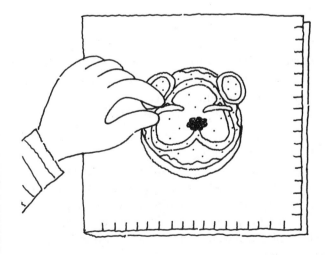

Add eyes, ears, and a nose.

Shhh! Don't wake the bear!

Hello, Groundhog!

Greet groundhog on his special day with this fruity critter snack.

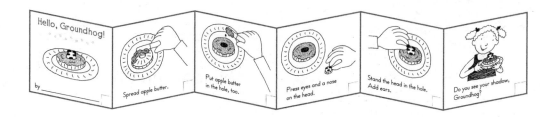

Ingredients
(for each child)

- pineapple ring
- apple butter
- $\frac{1}{2}$-inch-thick round slice of banana
- 3 raisins
- 2 red grape quarters

Tools & Materials
(for each child)

- mini-book pattern (page 27)
- 6-inch paper or plastic plate
- plastic knife

Introducing the Snack

Introduce children to the legend of Groundhog Day: If the groundhog sees his shadow on February 2, winter will last another six weeks; if he does not see his shadow, spring will soon arrive. Then invite children to discuss whether or not they think a groundhog's behavior can actually predict the weather. After sharing, tell them that they will make a fruity groundhog treat. Finally, have them make the corresponding mini-book.

Ahead of Time

- If using canned pineapple rings, drain them thoroughly before making the snack.
- Cut each grape in half lengthwise and again crosswise to make four ears. One grape can be used for every two children.

Helpful Tip

Show children how to gently press the raisin eyes and nose onto the banana head. The raisins should remain in place when the head is placed upright in the opening of the pineapple ring.

Extending the Learning

Print the word *groundhog* on chart paper. Explain that this word is a compound word—a word made up of two or more smaller words. Point out the two words in *groundhog* and circle each one. Then invite children to brainstorm other compound words, such as *cupcake*, *rainbow*, *shoestring*, and *hairbrush*. Write each of their responses on the chart. Read each word aloud with children, then have a volunteer circle the words that make up that compound word.

Hello, Groundhog!

by _____

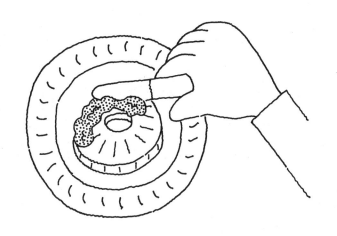

Spread apple butter.

Glue page 3 here.

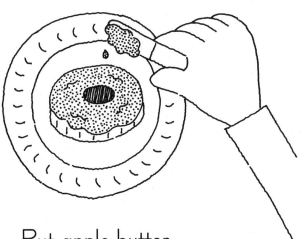

Put apple butter
in the hole, too.

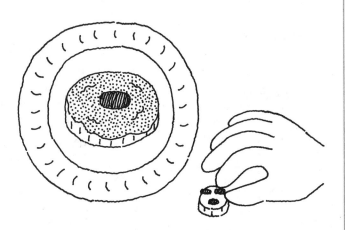

Press eyes and a nose
on the head.

Glue page 5 here.

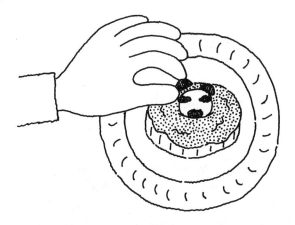

Stand the head in the hole.
Add ears.

Do you see your shadow,
Groundhog?

Fruity Heart Delight

Kids will love the sweetheart flavors of this delicious Valentine!

Introducing the Snack

Valentine's Day is a time to show others that you care for and appreciate them. Invite children to share some ways in which they can let the special people in their lives know how much they care. Their responses might include making a handmade Valentine's Day card, doing a good deed, spending time together, or simply telling that special person how they feel. After discussing, tell children that they will create a special Valentine's Day snack just for themselves. Afterward, invite them to make the corresponding mini-book.

Ahead of Time

- Cut $\frac{3}{8}$-inch to $\frac{1}{2}$-inch thick slices from the apple on opposite sides of the core (avoid the seeds).
- Choose strawberries that have a heart-like shape. Then remove the caps and cut the strawberries into slices about $\frac{3}{16}$-inch thick to represent small hearts.

Helpful Tips

- As needed, help children use the cookie cutter to cut out a heart shape from the apple slice.
- Show children how to flatten the cupcake liner before placing the apple heart on it.

Ingredients
(for each child)

- apple slice
- $\frac{1}{2}$ teaspoon low-fat strawberry yogurt
- strawberry slice
- dried cranberries

Tools & Materials
(for each child)

- mini-book pattern (page 29)
- $2\frac{1}{4}$-inch heart-shaped cookie cutter
- paper cupcake liner
- plastic spoon

Extending the Learning

Write *valentine* and other words related to Valentine's Day on heart cutouts. Include one-, two-, and three-syllable words, such as *sweetheart*, *candy*, *together*, *love*, *beautiful*, *card*, and *always*. Then choose one cutout at a time and read the word slowly, emphasizing each syllable. Ask children to repeat the word with you, clapping out the syllables they hear as they pronounce the word. How many syllables did they count? After reviewing all of the words, challenge children to sort the words on the cutouts into groups by syllable count.

Follow-the-Directions: No-Cook Snacks © 2012 by Immacula A. Rhodes, Scholastic Teaching Resources

Fruity Heart Delight

by _____

Cut out a heart.

Put it on a cupcake liner.

Spread yogurt.

Add a small heart and cranberries.

Happy Valentine's Day!

Glue page 3 here.

Glue page 5 here.

Lincoln's Log Cabin

Good nutrition is built right into this healthy President's Day snack.

Ingredients
(for each child)

- slice of wheat bread
- peanut butter
- 1 waffle-shaped pretzel
- pretzel sticks
- 3 pieces of Wheat Chex® cereal

Tools & Materials
(for each child)

- mini-book pattern (page 31)
- napkin
- plastic knife

Introducing the Snack

Who is Abraham Lincoln? Pose this question to children and have them share what they know about the 16th President of the United States. Then read aloud *Abe Lincoln: The Boy Who Loved Books* by Kay Winters (Simon & Schuster Books for Young Readers, 2003) or another book of your choice to share more about this great president. Afterward, tell children that they will make a log cabin treat to celebrate President's Day. Finally, invite them to make the corresponding mini-book.

Ahead of Time

Precut each slice of bread, cutting off the top corners, as shown on the recipe card. (See page 31.)

Helpful Tips

- Show children how to break the pretzel sticks into pieces and place them to fit around and above the door.
- If desired, substitute almond butter for peanut butter.

Extending the Learning

What letter does *Lincoln* begin with? After children respond correctly, help them brainstorm other words that begin with *L*, such as *lamb*, *leg*, *little*, *log*, *laugh*, and *light*. Record the words on chart paper. Then give children several half-sheets of paper pre-trimmed to resemble a simple log cabin shape. Have them write a few *L* words on each page and draw pictures for those that can be illustrated. Finally, help children bind their pages into a book, draw a log cabin on the front cover, and add the title "My *L* Log Cabin."

Lincoln's Log Cabin

by _____

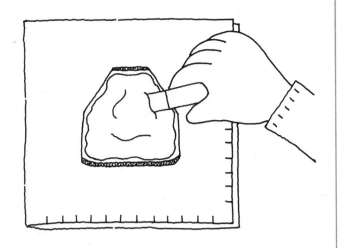

Spread peanut butter.

Glue page 3 here.

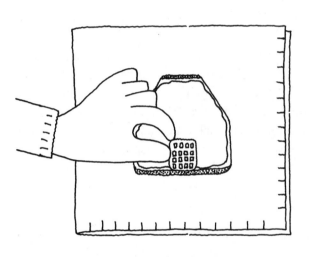

Place the door.

Add the logs.

Glue page 5 here.

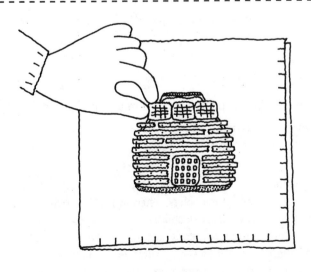

Put on the roof.

It's yummy! Honest!

Veggie Shamrock

This yummy shamrock is chock-full of nutritious greens.

Ingredients
(for each child)

◆ 3 round zucchini slices

◆ avocado spread

◆ chopped green bell pepper

◆ chopped celery

◆ green bell pepper strip

Tools & Materials
(for each child)

◆ mini-book pattern (page 33)

◆ napkin

◆ plastic knife

Introducing the Snack

Introduce children to vocabulary, traditions, and symbols related to St. Patrick's Day. Point out that shamrocks, or three-leaf clovers, are a common symbol of the March 17 celebration. Then invite children to share about how they observe St. Patrick's Day. Afterward, tell them that they will create a special shamrock snack that uses only green ingredients! When finished, invite children to make the corresponding mini-book.

Ahead of Time

◆ Cut the zucchini into $\frac{3}{8}$-inch round slices.

◆ For the avocado spread, peel and pit an avocado, cut it into small pieces, then mash the pieces into a soft pulp. One avocado can be used for eight to ten children.

◆ Chop the bell pepper and celery into small pieces.

◆ Cut a $\frac{1}{4}$- by 2-inch strip of bell pepper for each child to use as a stem.

Helpful Tips

◆ Invite children to help you mash the avocado to make the spread.

◆ If desired, use a pre-prepared avocado dip for the spread.

Extending the Learning

To provide practice in reading color words, label shamrock cutouts *green*, *red*, *blue*, *yellow*, and so on. (If children are learning their colors, you might write each color word on a shamrock in the matching color.) To use, ask children to read the word on each shamrock and identify objects around the room that match the color. Later, put the shamrocks and a collection of small, colored items in a center. Have children sort the items by color, placing each group with its corresponding color word.

Veggie Shamrock

by _____

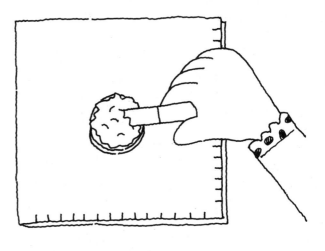

Spread avocado.

Glue page 3 here.

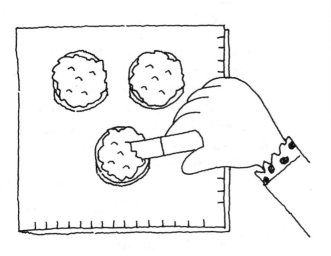

Make two more leaves.

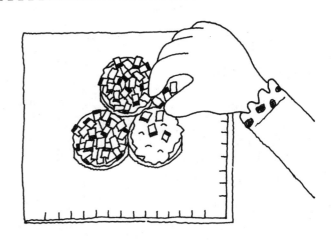

Put the leaves together.
Sprinkle on veggies.

Glue page 5 here.

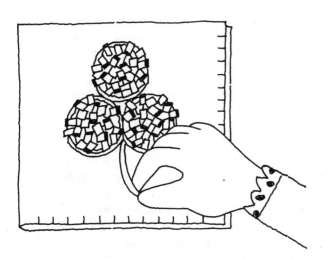

Add a stem.

Green is great!

High-Flying Kite

This cracker-based kite is a breeze to make.

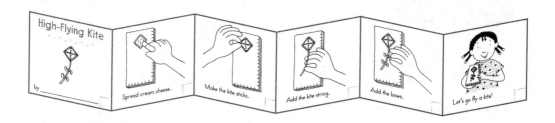

Ingredients
(for each child)

- saltine cracker
- cream cheese spread
- sunflower seeds
- thin celery strip
- cashew halves

Tools & Materials
(for each child)

- mini-book pattern (page 35)
- dinner napkin
- plastic knife

Introducing the Snack

Invite children to share about their experiences with the wind. How does the wind feel when it blows in their face? Have they ever chased something that was blown away by the wind? Have they ever tried to fly a kite? As you discuss the wind, point out that spring is often associated with breezy days and flying kites. Then invite children to make this quick-and-easy kite snack to celebrate windy spring days. Afterward, have them make the corresponding mini-book.

Ahead of Time

- Cut thin strips of celery in lengths of about four inches each to use for the kite strings.
- Fold the napkins in half.

Helpful Tips

- If desired, use a flavored cream cheese spread, such as garden vegetable, sundried tomato & basil, or spinach & artichoke, to add more color and flavor to the snack.
- For the bowties, you might substitute small triangles cut from Swiss cheese slices for the cashew halves.

Extending the Learning

List single-syllable, long-vowel words that end with silent e on chart paper. Include words for the vowels *a*, *i*, *o*, and *u*; for example, *bake*, *dime*, *rope*, and *cube*. Point to and say each word. Ask children to name the vowel they hear. Then have them name the vowel they see, but can't hear when saying the word (the final *e*). Explain that in these words, the first vowel "talks" while the final *e* remains silent. Finally, challenge children to search print around the room to find other silent-*e* words to add to the list.

High-Flying Kite

by _____

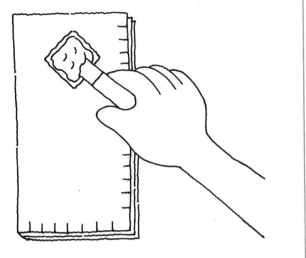

Spread cream cheese.

Glue page 3 here.

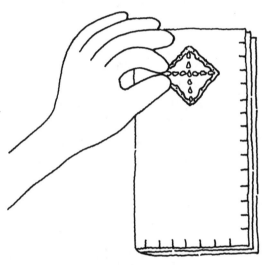

Make the kite sticks.

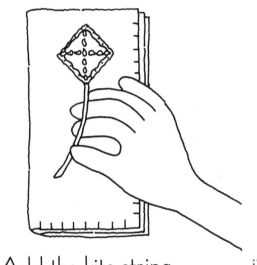

Add the kite string.

Glue page 5 here.

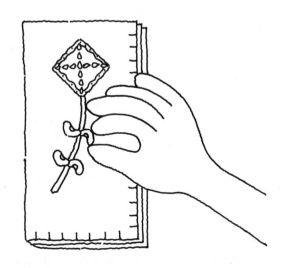

Add the bows.

Let's go fly a kite!

April Shower

This rainy-day snack will bring a smile to kids' faces!

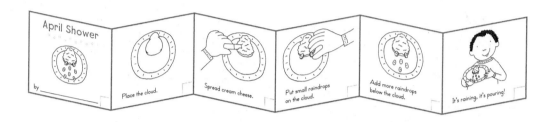

Ingredients
(for each child)

◆ 1 pear half

◆ 1 tablespoon whipped cream cheese spread

◆ thin white grape slices

Tools & Materials
(for each child)

◆ mini-book pattern (page 37)

◆ 9-inch paper or plastic plate

◆ plastic knife

Introducing the Snack

Review with children the three processes of the water cycle: evaporation, condensation, and precipitation. Explain that the water cycle is nature's way of recycling rain. Then describe how the three processes work together to recycle rain, emphasizing the role of clouds in the cycle. Afterward, tell children that they will make a fruity rain cloud to enjoy for snack. Finally, have them make the corresponding mini-book.

Ahead of Time

◆ Peel and cut each pear in half, removing the seeds from the halves. One pear can be used for every two children.

◆ If using canned pears, drain them thoroughly before making the snack.

◆ Cut the grapes lengthwise into thin slices to make the raindrops.

Helpful Tips

◆ If desired, create a storm cloud by mixing a drop or two of blackberry juice in the whipped cream cheese spread to give it a grayish-purple color.

◆ You might use a blue plate as a background to represent the sky.

Extending the Learning

Label four white cloud cutouts with the diphthongs *oi*, *ou*, *ow*, and *oy*. Then write words that are spelled with each of the diphthongs on light blue raindrop cutouts. Words you might use include *cloud*, *mouth*, *house*, *choice*, *point*, *soil*, *brown*, *howl*, *now*, *boy*, *joy*, and *toy*. After reviewing the words with children and pointing out the diphthong pairs *oi/oy*, and *ou/ow*, place the clouds and raindrops in a learning center. Invite children to read and then sort the words by their vowel spellings, placing each one with the corresponding cloud.

April Shower

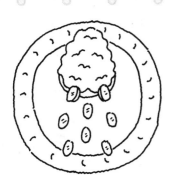

by _____

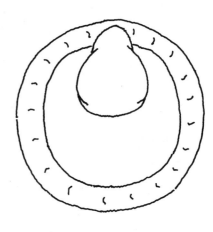

Place the cloud.

Glue page 3 here.

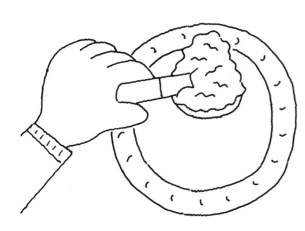

Spread cream cheese.

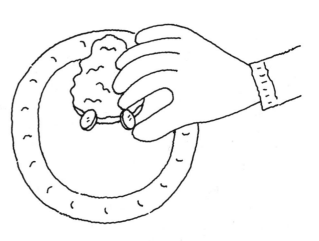

Put small raindrops on the cloud.

Glue page 5 here.

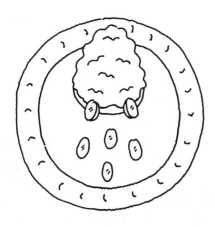

Add more raindrops below the cloud.

It's raining, it's pouring!

Tulip Garden

Kids' taste buds will bloom with this garden full of flowers.

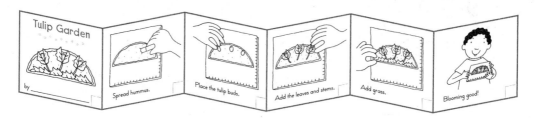

Ingredients
(for each child)

◆ $\frac{1}{2}$ eight-inch whole-wheat flour tortilla

◆ hummus

◆ 3 grape tomato halves

◆ 3 baby spinach leaves (with stems)

◆ small pieces of lettuce

Tools & Materials
(for each child)

◆ mini-book pattern (page 39)

◆ napkin

◆ plastic knife

Introducing the Snack

Talk with children about the basic needs of plants: soil, water, and light. Explain that each of these things is necessary to help plants grow healthy and strong. Then name the different stages of plant growth, from seed to mature plant. Display pictures of plants and point out the different parts, such as roots, stems, leaves, and blooms. Conclude by telling children that they will make a tulip garden snack—from foods that came from plants! Afterward, have children make the corresponding mini-book.

Ahead of Time

◆ Cut small grape tomatoes in half lengthwise to make the tulip buds. Three tomatoes can be used for every two children.

◆ Split each spinach leaf down the center starting at the tip and ending at the stem. (Keep the stem intact.)

◆ Tear lettuce leaves into small pieces for use as grass.

Helpful Tips

◆ If desired, substitute a multi-grain tortilla for the whole-wheat one.

◆ Show children how to gently spread the two sides of the spinach leaves while placing them over the tulip buds.

◆ Choose green lettuce that has ragged edges for the grass.

Grow children's word skills with a flower-garden word wall. Label large flower cutouts with garden-related words, such as *dig, plant, grow, bloom,* and *rain.* Leave space on the flowers to write other words around the feature word. Then read each word aloud and have children brainstorm words that belong to the same word family. For *dig* they might say, *big, pig,* and *wig.* Write their responses on the flower. After presenting each word, add leafy stems and display the flowers on a word wall. Encourage children to use words from the display in their plant-related writing activities.

Tulip Garden

by _____

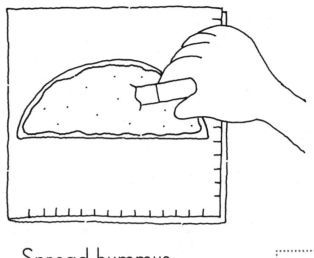

Spread hummus.

Glue page 3 here.

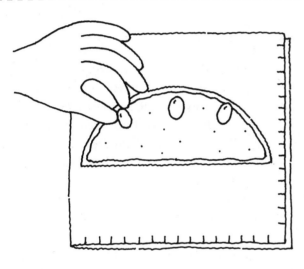

Place the tulip buds.

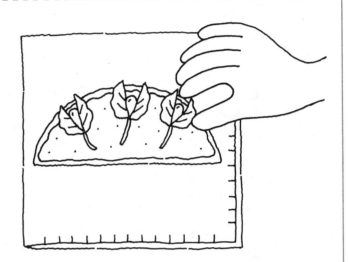

Add the leaves and stems.

Glue page 5 here.

Add grass.

Blooming good!

Baby Chick

Children will chirp with delight over this little bird snack.

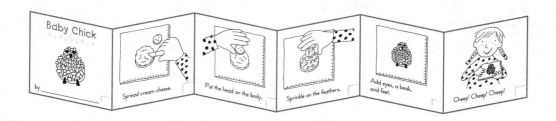

Ingredients
(for each child)

- small round slice of squash
- large round slice of squash
- 1 tablespoon whipped cream cheese spread
- chopped yellow bell pepper
- 3 small carrot triangles
- 2 small pieces of carrot

Tools & Materials
(for each child)

- mini-book pattern (page 41)
- napkin
- plastic knife

Introducing the Snack

Newly hatched chicks are often used to symbolize spring and the new life that begins during this season. Ask children to name some animals that hatch from eggs. Did they include animals such as turtles, snakes, fish, and lizards? Point out that birds are not the only animals that come from eggs. After sharing, tell children that they will make a cute, yellow chick for snack. When finished, invite them to make the corresponding mini-book.

Ahead of Time

- Cut the small slice of squash (about $\frac{1}{4}$-inch thick) from the neck of a yellow crookneck squash. Cut the large slice from the body of the squash.
- To make "feathers," chop the yellow bell pepper into small pieces.
- Cut small triangles from carrot slices for the chick's beak and feet. Cut additional, small pieces of carrots to use for the eyes.

Helpful Tip

If desired, substitute a cheddar cheese spread for the cream cheese spread.

Extending the Learning

Write *chick* and *cheep* on the chalkboard. Read both words aloud, pointing out the letters at the beginning of the words and the sound they make. Then ask children to brainstorm other words that begin with *ch*. Write their responses on the board. Then, to reinforce children's listening skills, have them pretend to be chicks. Tell them that you will call out one word at a time. If the word begins with *ch*, the chicks will respond by cheeping. If not, the chicks will remain quiet.

Baby Chick

by _____

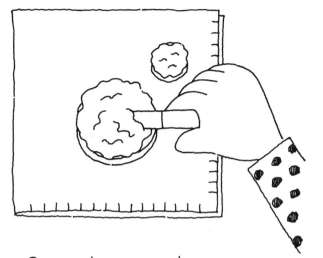

Spread cream cheese.

Glue page 3 here.

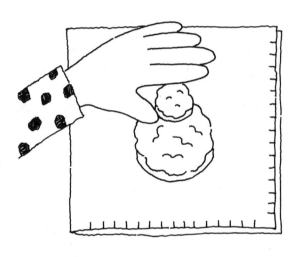

Put the head on the body.

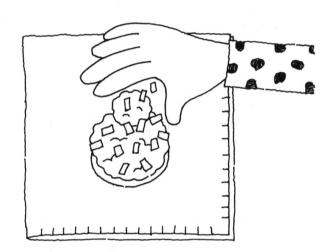

Sprinkle on the feathers.

Glue page 5 here.

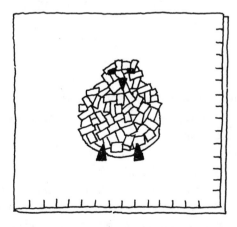

Add eyes, a beak, and feet.

Cheep! Cheep! Cheep!

Pond Turtle

This turtle treat is totally tasty—shell, tail, and all!

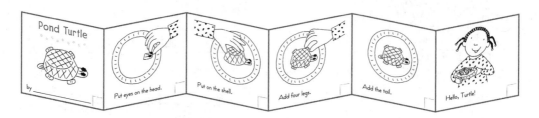

Ingredients
(for each child)

- 2-inch length of banana tip, cut in half lengthwise
- 2 raisins
- waffle cup
- two $\frac{1}{2}$-inch wide banana slices, each cut in half
- $\frac{1}{2}$-inch length of banana tip, cut in half lengthwise

Tools & Materials
(for each child)

- mini-book pattern (page 43)
- 6-inch paper plate

Introducing the Snack

Explain that all kinds of animals live in or near ponds. Display pictures of different pond animals, such as fish, ducks, frogs, mice, and turtles. Then discuss the characteristics of each animal, guiding children to understand which animal group it belongs to: fish, bird, amphibian, mammal, or reptile. Afterward, tell children they will make a special turtle snack with a crunchy shell. Finally, have children make the corresponding mini-book.

Ahead of Time

- For the turtle heads, cut each 2-inch length of banana tip in half lengthwise. Each piece will make two heads. Cut each $\frac{1}{2}$-inch length of banana tip in the same manner to create the turtle tails.
- After using both tips of a banana, you can make additional head and tail pieces by cutting $2\frac{1}{2}$-inch slices from the remaining length of the fruit, then rounding one end of each section to resemble the tip of the banana. Cut these sections in half lengthwise, as described above.
- Cut the $\frac{1}{2}$-inch wide banana slices in half, creating semicircles to use for the legs.

Helpful Tip

Have children place the rim of the waffle cup over the middle of the banana head. Show them how to gently press the cup into the banana so that it sinks into the piece but does not cut it in two.

Extending the Learning

Label a supply of turtle cutouts with pond-related words such as *duck*, *fish*, *grass*, *toad*, *swim*, and *water*. Review the words with children. Then pair up children and give four to five cutouts to each pair. On a signal, have children arrange their words in alphabetical order. Once done, have each pair check another pair's work. Ask them to work together to correct any words that are out of order.

Pond Turtle

by _____

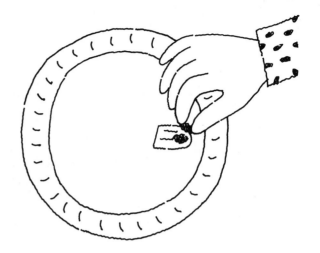

Put eyes on the head.

Glue page 3 here.

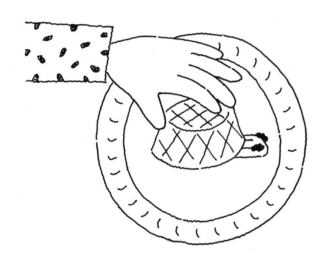

Put on the shell.

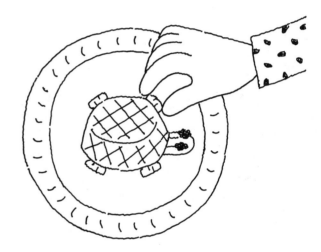

Add four legs.

Glue page 5 here.

Add the tail.

Hello, Turtle!

Dandelion Puff

The mix of flavors in this snack makes a dandy treat!

Introducing the Snack

Have children ever picked a dandelion to blow the puff of seeds away? Invite them to share their experiences. Then read aloud *A Dandelion's Life* by John Himmelman (Children's Press, 1998). Afterward, ask children to speculate about what might have happened to the dandelion seeds that they've blown away. Conclude by telling them that they will make a special dandelion snack to enjoy. Finally, have children make the corresponding mini-book.

Ingredients
(for each child)

- round cucumber slice
- cream cheese spread
- unsweetened shredded coconut
- thin celery strip
- 2 arugula leaves

Tools & Materials
(for each child)

- mini-book pattern (page 45)
- napkin
- plastic knife

Ahead of Time

- Cut cucumbers into $\frac{3}{8}$-inch-thick slices.
- Put the coconut in a bowl so children can more easily spoon out enough to use as puff seeds on their dandelion.
- Cut celery into thin, $2\frac{1}{2}$-inch long strips to use for the dandelion stems.

Helpful Tip

If available at your local food market, you might use actual dandelion greens instead of arugula leaves. (Avoid picking wild dandelion greens due to the possibility that chemicals have been used on them!)

Dandelions are one of the most common—and most irresistible—plants around. Take advantage of children's natural attraction to these plants with this comprehension activity. First, label large, plain index cards with simple action sentences related to dandelions, such as "Blow on a dandelion," "Pick a dandelion," and "Shake a dandelion." Give one child at a time a card to read (silently) and then act out the sentence. Ask classmates to guess the action being performed. Finally, have the child read the sentence aloud.

Dandelion Puff

by _____

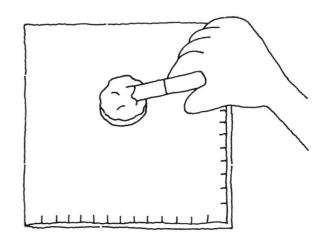

Spread cream cheese.

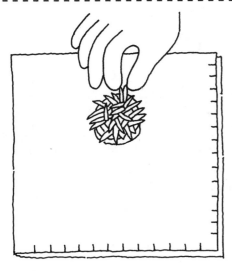

Sprinkle on puff seeds.

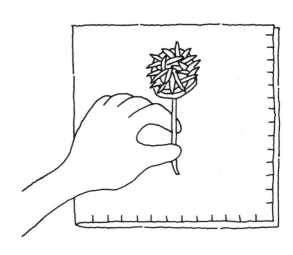

Add a stem.

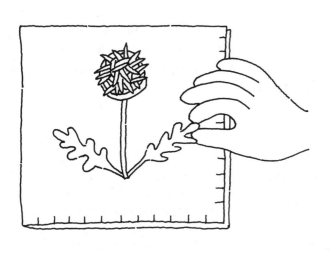

Add leaves.

1, 2, 3, blow!

Busy Beehive

Kids will be all a-buzz about building this beehive snack.

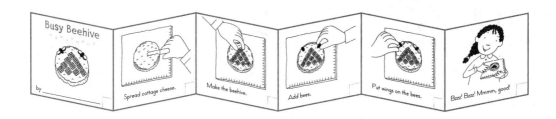

Ingredients

(for each child)

- rice cake
- 10 pieces of Kellogg's® Crispix® cereal
- cottage cheese
- 2 raisins
- 4 blanched almond slices

Tools & Materials

(for each child)

- mini-book pattern (page 47)
- napkin
- plastic knife

Introducing the Snack

Ask children to name what kind of animal lives in a hive. Once they give the correct response (*bees*), challenge children to name other animals and their homes. They might include bears and dens, ants and anthills, rabbits and burrows, and birds and nests. After sharing, tell children that they will build a beehive treat along with a few bees to enjoy for snack. Then have them make the corresponding mini-book.

Ahead of Time

For younger children, you might group together the 10 pieces of cereal for each child.

Helpful Tips

- Let children practice putting the almond wings and raisin body together before they make the bees on the rice cake.
- If desired, substitute cream cheese spread or low-fat plain yogurt for the cottage cheese.

Cut out a supply of hexagons and label each one with a word that contains a long vowel pair, such as *ai*, *ay*, *ee*, *ea*, *oa*, *oe*, *ue*, and *ui*. Put the shapes in a paper bag. Then label five plain index cards with "long *a*," "long *e*," and so on. Space the cards evenly across the top of a table. To use, have children take turns removing a hexagon from the bag, reading the word, then placing it below the corresponding long vowel card. As children add hexagons, have them arrange the pieces into the shape of a beehive.

Follow-the-Directions: No-Cook Snacks © 2012 by Immacula A. Rhodes, Scholastic Teaching Resources

Busy Beehive

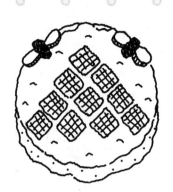

by _____

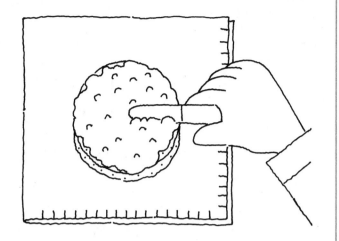

Spread cottage cheese.

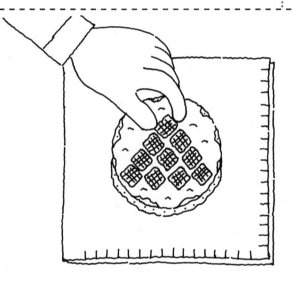

Make the beehive.

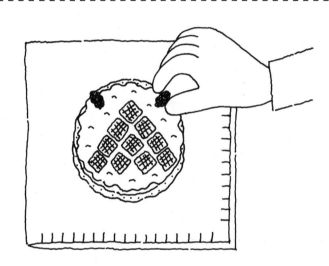

Add bees.

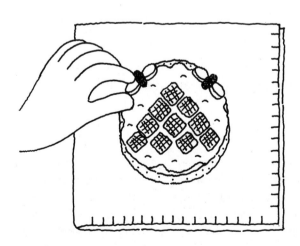

Put wings on the bees.

Bzzz! Bzzz! Mmmm, good!

Patriotic Star

Red, white, and blue have never tasted so good!

Ingredients
(for each child)

- slice of seedless watermelon
- $\frac{1}{2}$-inch thick slice of apple
- 1 teaspoon low-fat vanilla yogurt
- blueberry

Tools & Materials
(for each child)

- mini-book pattern (page 49)
- 6-inch paper or plastic plate
- large star-shaped cookie cutter
- small star-shaped cookie cutter
- 1 plastic spoon

Introducing the Snack

Challenge children to name a patriotic symbol that has the colors red, white, and blue. Did they name the American flag? Explain that the American flag is a common sight in July 4th celebrations—a time when Americans celebrate their country and freedom. Show children a flag and talk about what the colors, stars, and stripes on it symbolize. Afterward, tell children they will celebrate Independence Day by making a patriotic star snack. Then have them make the corresponding mini-book.

Ahead of Time

- Cut a $\frac{1}{2}$-inch thick slice of watermelon for each child, making it large enough for children to use for the large star.
- Cut $\frac{1}{2}$-inch thick slices from the apple on opposite sides of the core (avoid the seeds) for children to use for the small star.

Helpful Tip

As needed, help children use the cookie cutters to cut out the star shapes from the watermelon and apple slices.

Extending the Learning

Write *star* on chart paper. Ask children to read the word and tell what vowel sound they hear in it. After exploring the possible sounds—such as long or short *a*—point out that the *r* in the word changes the sound of the vowel. Write other words that have *r*-controlled vowels, such as *shirt*, *fur*, and *corn* and point out that the *r* controls the vowel sound in those words. Finally, work with children to brainstorm other words with *r*-controlled vowels to add to the chart. When finished, randomly point to words on the chart, calling on volunteers to read them.

Patriotic Star

by _____

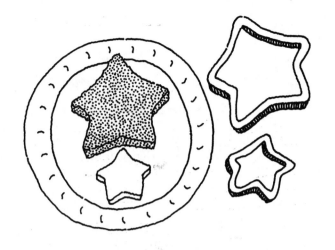

Cut out the stars.

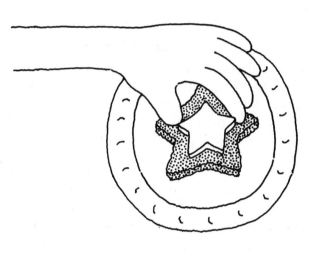

Stack the stars.

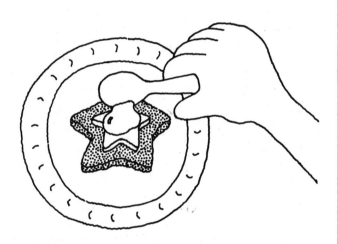

Put on yogurt.

Add a blueberry.

Hooray for red, white, and blue!

Cool Summer Sipper

This fruity, refreshing drink is perfect for hot summer days.

Ingredients

(for each child)

- $\frac{1}{4}$ cup low-fat vanilla yogurt
- pinch of cinnamon powder
- $\frac{1}{2}$ cup orange juice
- orange slice

Tools & Materials

(for each child)

- mini-book pattern (page 51)
- 2 plastic measuring cups
- clear plastic cup
- plastic spoon

Introducing the Snack

Ask children to share what they know about being safe in the hot, summer sun. After sharing, list on chart paper some general safety rules they can follow while enjoying the outdoors; for instance, drink plenty of water and other fluids, put on sunscreen, and wear a hat and sunglasses. If desired, invite volunteers to illustrate the chart, then display it near the door in your classroom. Afterward, tell children that they will make an orange-flavored sipper to enjoy for snack. Finally, have them make the corresponding mini-book.

Ahead of Time

- Label each measuring cup with "yogurt" or "orange juice." Tell children which cup to use for each ingredient.
- For younger children, you might pre-measure the yogurt and orange juice into separate paper cups for each child.
- Cut oranges into thin slices, then slit each one so that it fits easily onto the rim of the cup.

Helpful Tip

- Show children how to mix the cinnamon thoroughly with the yogurt. Mixing well will prevent the powder from rising to the top once the orange juice is added.
- If desired, substitute banana-flavored yogurt for the vanilla yogurt.

Ask children to tell what beginning letter they hear in the phrase "summer sipper." After they respond, present other alliterative phrases and have children identify the repeating beginning sounds. Then invite them to choose a letter to use when making up their own alliterative phrases. The phrases can be silly or serious, such as "big brown bear," "eleven elves eating," "purple pig pants," and "ten tall tents." Silly or not, have children draw pictures to go with their phrases. When finished, have them share their work with the class.

Cool Summer Sipper

by _____

Put in yogurt.

Glue page 3 here.

Add cinnamon and mix well.

Stir in orange juice.

Glue page 5 here.

Put on orange slice.

Refreshing!

Ladybug on a Leaf

This ladybug is fresh enough to fly straight in from the garden!

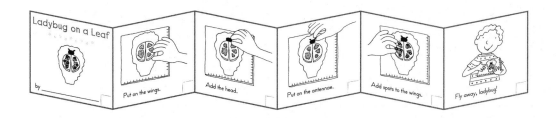

Introducing the Snack

Tell children that a ladybug is an insect. Then explain that insects have three body sections (a head, thorax, and abdomen), six legs, antennae, and most have wings. Invite children to name as many insects as they can. If they mention spiders, take the opportunity to point out the differences between insects and arachnids. Afterward, tell children that they will be making a ladybug snack from foods that can be grown in a garden. Then have them make the corresponding mini-book.

Ahead of Time

- Cut each tomato slice in half to make a pair of wings for each child.
- Cut the large black olive in half lengthwise to make two ladybug heads. One olive can be used for every two children.
- Cut small olives into slices for spots.
- Cut olive slices into short strips to use for the antennae.

Helpful Tip

Show children how to place the wings so that they touch at the top and are spread apart slightly at the bottom.

Ingredients
(for each child)

- large lettuce leaf
- tomato slice, cut in half
- $\frac{1}{2}$ extra-large black olive
- small black olive slices
- short black olive strips

Tools & Materials
(for each child)

- mini-book pattern (page 53)
- napkin

Point out the ingredient in this recipe that starts with a vowel: *olives*. Ask children to tell what vowel the word begins with. Then create and label a five-column chart with the five vowels. Work with children to brainstorm words that begin with vowels, listing each word in the column corresponding to the vowel it begins with. Later, invite children to make a mini-book for the vowel of their choice. Have them write a word that begins with their vowel on each page and then illustrate the word (if possible) or write a sentence with it.

Ladybug on a Leaf

by _____

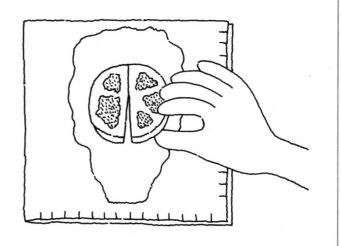

Put on the wings.

Glue page 3 here.

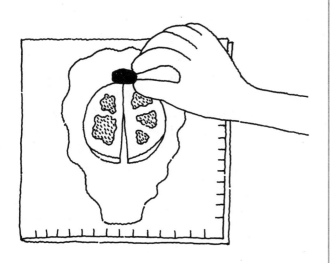

Add the head.

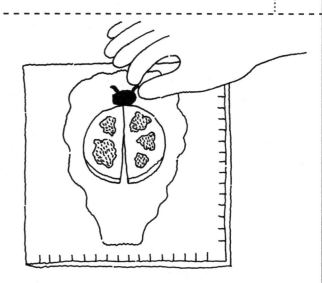

Put on the antennae.

Glue page 5 here.

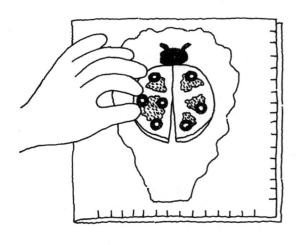

Add spots to the wings.

Fly away, ladybug!

Delicious Fish

This yummy fish will make a big splash with kids.

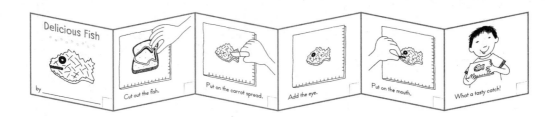

Delicious Fish

by _____

Cut out the fish.

Put on the carrot spread.

Add the eye.

Put on the mouth.

What a tasty catch!

Ingredients
(for each child)

- slice of whole-wheat bread
- carrot spread
- green olive slice
- short strip of red bell pepper

Tools & Materials
(for each child)

- mini-book pattern (page 55)
- fish-shaped cookie cutter
- napkin
- plastic knife

Introducing the Snack

What has scales, gills, and lives under water? Fish! After children respond, display several pictures of fish along with a few water mammals, such as whales and dolphins. Ask children if all of the pictured animals are fish. Encourage them to examine the animals closely for scales and gills. Point out that some underwater animals resemble fish, but are mammals. Finally, compare the characteristics of fish and mammals. Then tell children they will make a fish treat to enjoy for snack. Afterward, have them make the corresponding mini-book.

Ahead of Time

Make the carrot spread by mixing finely grated carrot with Greek yogurt until it reaches a consistency that can be spread easily. In general, one heaping teaspoon of grated carrot mixed with one level teaspoon of Greek yogurt makes enough carrot spread for one child.

Helpful Tips

- As needed, help children use the cookie cutter to cut out a fish shape from the bread.
- If desired, substitute a pimento strip for the red bell pepper strip. (You can purchase green olives that contain pimento strips.)

Extending the Learning

Reinforce rhyming with this fill-in-the-blank activity. To begin, say a sentence starter such as "If I were a fish, I'd _____." Fill in the blank with a phrase that ends with a rhyming word for *fish*; for instance, "I'd live in a dish" or "I'd grant you a wish." Invite children to take turns repeating the sentence frame and filling in their own rhyming endings. Continue, using the names of other water animals in the sentence starter, such as "If I were a whale," "If I were a seal," and "If I were a crab."

Delicious Fish

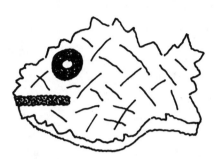

by _____

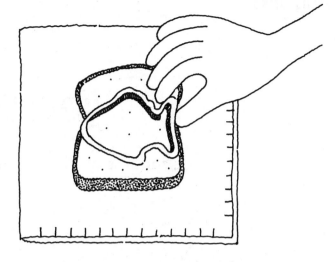

Cut out the fish.

Glue page 3 here.

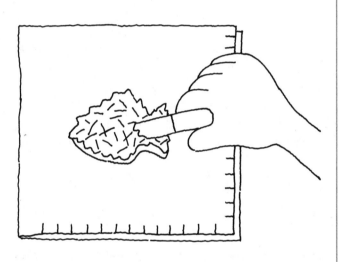

Put on the carrot spread.

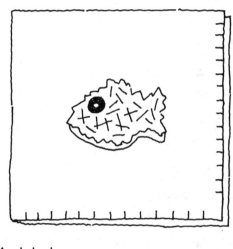

Add the eye.

Glue page 5 here.

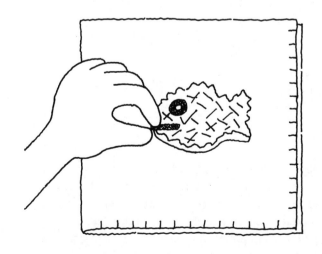

Put on the mouth.

What a tasty catch!

Veggie Me

This snack is nutritious, delicious, and uniquely "Me!"

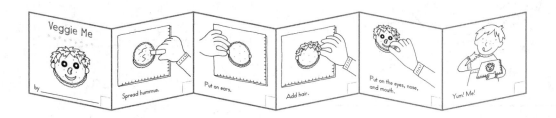

Ingredients
(for each child)

- rice cake
- hummus
- carrot slice, cut in half
- lettuce leaves
- black olive rings
- celery slice
- red bell pepper strip

Tools & Materials
(for each child)

- mini-book pattern (page 57)
- napkin
- plastic knife

Introducing the Snack

Tell children that we are all unique in our own ways. Then invite children to share the things that make them special and different from others. Encourage them to tell about the physical features that describe themselves, such as eye, hair, and skin color, as well as their likes, dislikes, favorite activities, and talents that help set them apart. Afterward, tell children that they will make a snack to represent themselves. Then have them make the corresponding mini-book.

Ahead of Time

- For ears, cut carrot slices in half to create semicircles. One carrot slice can be used for each child.
- Cut thin slices of celery for children to use for their nose.
- Cut curved strips of red bell pepper (about 1–2 inches long) to use as mouths.

Helpful Tip

Provide different types of lettuce for children to choose from to represent their hair texture and color.

Remind children that they are unique. In fact, some of them may be opposites of each other. For example, some children might be tall, while others are short. Or one child might have large feet and another small feet. Help children brainstorm other opposite pairs such as *hot/cold*, *empty/full*, and *open/closed*. Record each pair on chart paper. Then invite children to work with partners to make up sentences using each word in an opposite pair.

Veggie Me

by _____

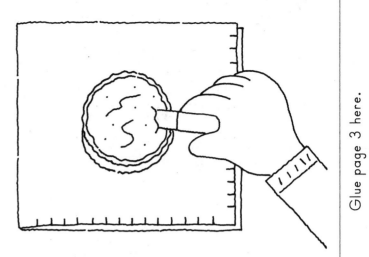

Spread hummus.

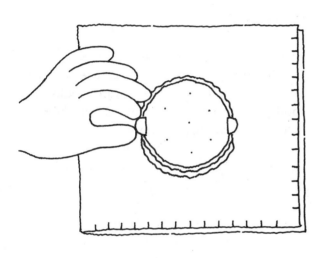

Put on ears.

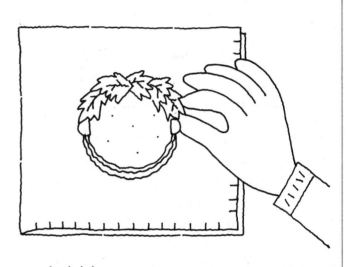

Add hair.

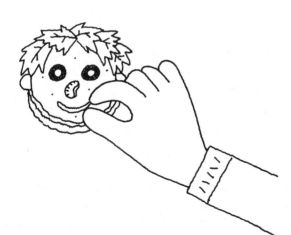

Put on the eyes, nose, and mouth.

Yum! Me!

"Berry" Happy Birthday

Here's a perfectly fruity treat that's great for celebrating kids' special day.

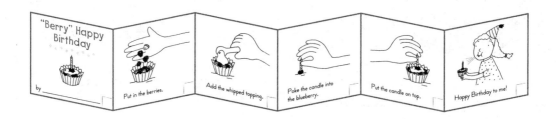

Ingredients
(for each child)

- variety of berries (such as blueberries, blackberries, raspberries, and strawberries)
- 1 tablespoon of light whipped topping

Tools & Materials
(for each child)

- mini-book pattern (page 59)
- foil or paper cupcake liner
- plastic spoon
- birthday candle

Introducing the Snack

Create a timeline, displaying the months of the year in sequence. Then ask children to find the month of their birthday. Help them write their name and the date of their special day on a plain index card to add to the timeline next to the appropriate month. Have children put their cards in numerical order wherever more than one card has been posted for a particular month. Finally, tell children that they will make a sweet treat to commemorate their special day. Afterward, have them make the corresponding mini-book.

Ahead of Time

- If using large strawberries, chop them into smaller pieces.
- Put each type of berry into separate dishes. Have spoons (or tongs) available for scooping out the berries.

Helpful Tips

- Provide napkins for children to scoop their berries onto. Then they can put the berries into their cupcake liners by hand, mixing or layering the berries as they go.
- If desired, use a low-fat berry-flavored yogurt—such as blueberry, raspberry, or strawberry—instead of whipped topping.

Create a word card for each month of the year and day of the week. Use a different color for each set of words. Then hold up each card labeled with a day of the week and have children read the word. When finished, work with them to sequence the cards, starting with Sunday and ending with Saturday. Repeat with the cards labeled with the months of the year, having children sequence them from January to December. Later, place the cards in a learning center for children to do the activity independently.

"Berry" Happy Birthday

by _____

Put in the berries.

Glue page 3 here.

Add the whipped topping.

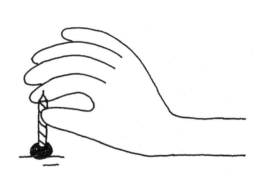

Poke the candle into the blueberry.

Glue page 5 here.

Put the candle on top.

Happy Birthday to me!

100th Day Treat

For a tasty, textured treat, this yummy snack really counts!

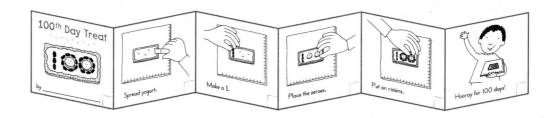

Ingredients

(for each child)

- graham cracker
- low-fat key lime yogurt
- 2 round banana slices
- raisins

Tools & Materials

(for each child)

- mini-book pattern (page 61)
- napkin
- plastic knife

Introducing the Snack

Count with children from 1 to 100 to celebrate the 100th day of school. You might count the days on a calendar, starting with the first day of school and ending on the day that marks the 100th day. Or count 100 small objects, shape cutouts, handclaps, or any other item or action that can be counted. Then tell children that they will make a snack to mark the 100th day of school. Afterward, have them make the corresponding mini-book.

Ahead of Time

Cut bananas into $\frac{3}{8}$-inch-thick slices.

Helpful Tips

If desired, substitute any yogurt flavor of your choice for the key lime yogurt. Be sure to choose a yogurt that is a color other than white or cream.

Extending the Learning

Prepare word cards for the numbers one through ten. Show each card to children and have them name the word. Then ask them to count up to that number, beginning with "one." After children are familiar with the number words, prepare a set of corresponding number cards. Place both sets of cards in a center along with a supply of counters. To use, have children match each number to its word card and then count out a set of counters to equal that quantity. To extend, ask them to put the card pairs and counter sets in numerical order.

100th Day Treat

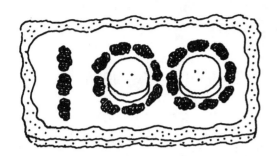

by _____

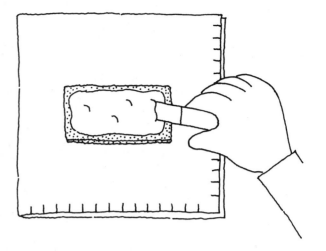

Spread yogurt.

Glue page 3 here.

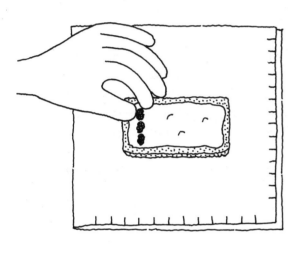

Make a 1.

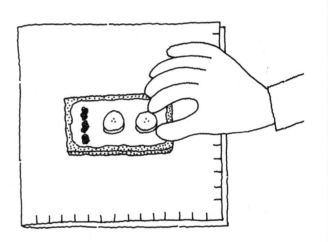

Place the zeroes.

Glue page 5 here.

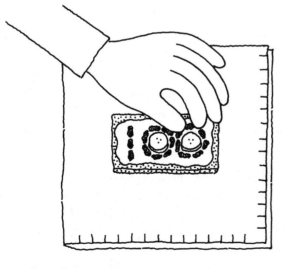

Put on raisins.

Hooray for 100 days!

Letter T-shirt

This fruit-flavored T-shirt is perfect for kids' snack-time appetite.

Ingredients
(for each child)

- slice of bread
- seedless, sugar-free blackberry jam
- oat cereal rings
- thin pieces of all-natural fruit strip

Tools & Materials
(for each child)

- mini-book pattern (page 63)
- napkin
- plastic knife

Introducing the Snack

Do children have a favorite T-shirt or other clothing item? Invite them to share about their favorite with the class and to explain why that particular article of clothing is so special. Is it a favorite color? Do they consider it lucky? Did a special family member make it or give it to them? Is it the most comfortable clothing item they own? After allowing plenty of time for sharing, tell children that they will make a T-shirt snack with their initial on it. Then have them make the corresponding mini-book.

Ahead of Time

For younger children, you might precut the bread into the shape of a T-shirt for each child.

Helpful Tips

- Show children how to cut out the T-shirt shape from the bread before they begin to make their snack.
- For the shirt trim, use thin strips cut from individually wrapped all-natural fruit strips, such as Stretch Island Fruit Co.™ Original Fruit Strips. You might provide mango-, apricot-, or apple-flavored fruit strips to add a contrasting color to the dark jam on the shirt.

Extending the Learning

Write your first and last initials on the board. Then ask children to brainstorm words beginning with each letter. Next, have them put together blank mini-books (see page 64). Ask them to write their first initial in large print at the top of the first page, their last initial on the next page, then their first initial, last initial, and so on until all the pages have been labeled. Finally, have them add words and drawings of things that begin with the letter on each page. Later, invite children to share their completed mini-books with partners.

Letter T-shirt

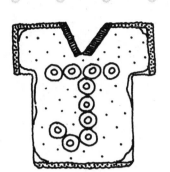

by _____

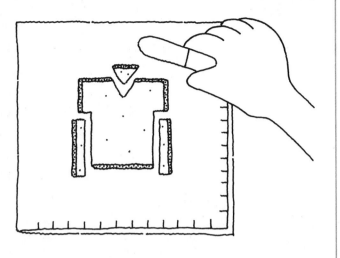

Cut out the T-shirt.

Glue page 3 here.

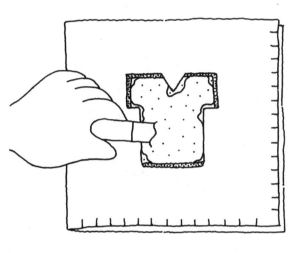

Spread the jam.

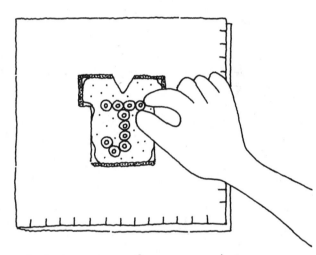

Make your first initial.

Glue page 5 here.

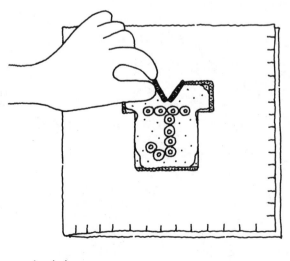

Add trim.

A stylish snack!

by _____

Glue page 3 here.

Glue page 5 here.

Follow-the-Directions: No-Cook Snacks © 2012 by
Immaculo A. Rhodes, Scholastic Teaching Resources • Page 64